Rachael's Adventure Trip

WRITTEN BY LINDA ANDREASSI

ILLUSTRATED BY OPPORTUNE PUBLISHING

This book is dedicated to all of those who have traveled or wish to travel.

Copyright © 2023 Linda Andreassi

All rights reserved. No part of this publication may be reproduced, distributed, or transmitted in any form or by any means, including photocopying, recording, or other electronic or mechanical methods, without the prior written permission of the publisher, except in the case of brief quotations embodied in critical reviews and certain other noncommercial uses permitted by copyright law. For permission requests, write to the publisher, addressed "Attention: Permissions Coordinator," at the address below.

Paperback ISBN: 978-1-63616-152-5
Hardcover ISBN: 978-1-63616-151-8

Published & Illustrated By Opportune Independent Publishing Company

Rachael and her mother strolled eagerly towards the airport, excited to meet her distant relatives.

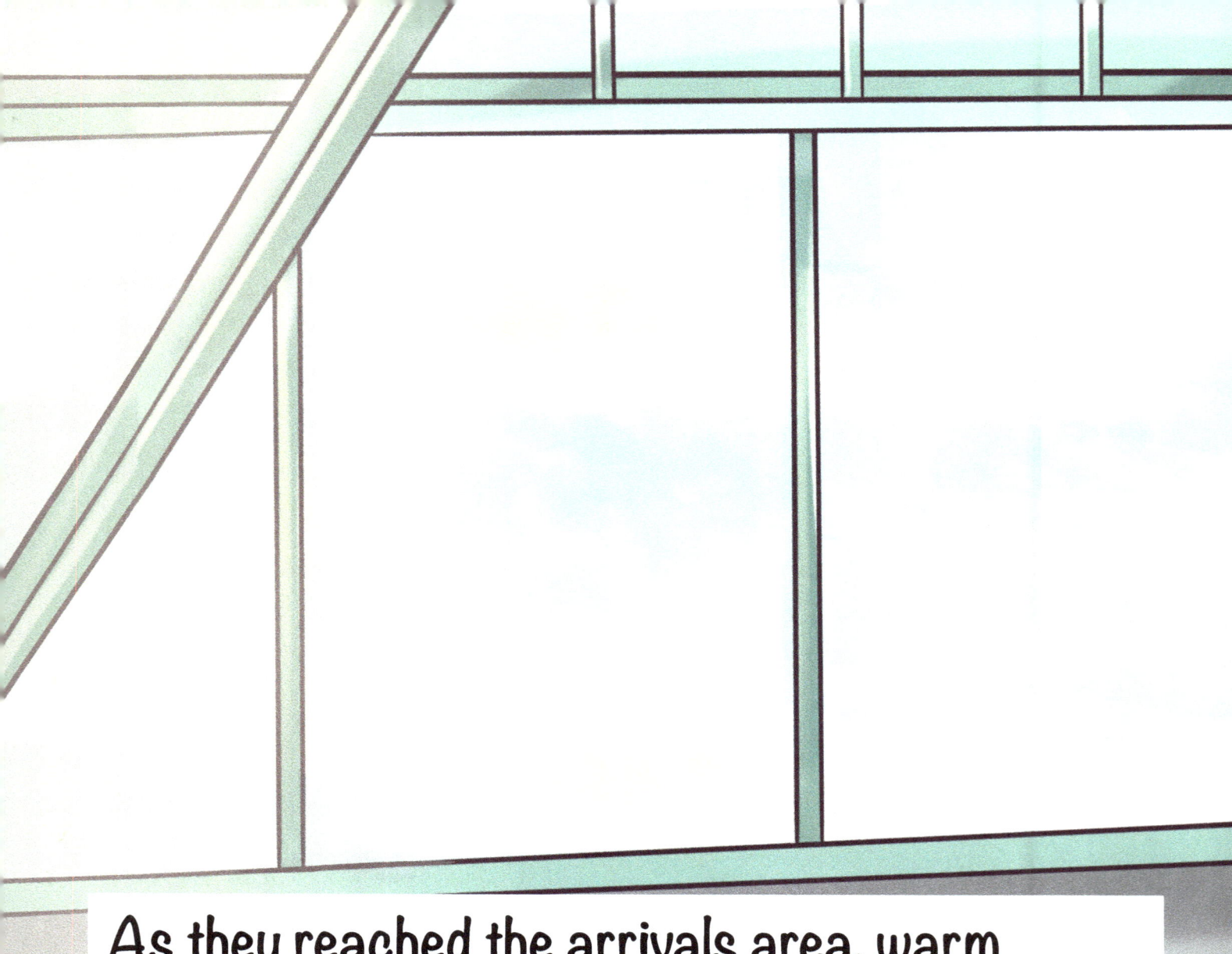

As they reached the arrivals area, warm embraces and smiles awaited them. The joy of meeting her extended family filled Rachael's heart as they exchanged greetings.

Eager to begin her adventure, Rachael's journey commenced with a leisurely bus ride transporting her and her family to a charming small town called Poggiofiorito, renowned as the village of flowers.

Upon reaching the destination, Rachael and her mother took a short walk to her cousin's house, accompanied by cool and breezy weather that made the experience delightful.

As Rachael entered her cousin's home, she was amazed by the number of people in the village who were related to her.

She indulged herself so much that her stomach ached, but the satisfaction was worth it.

After a satisfying meal and some much-needed rest, Rachael drifted off to sleep, her dreams filled with visions of the exciting places she would visit and the people she would meet.

The next morning, her family took her to a picturesque farm, where she marveled at the sight of grapevines, olive trees, lemon trees, fig trees, and peach trees. Rachael's love for lemonade was satisfied with a refreshing homemade glass made from the farm's lemons, while the juicy, sweet peaches delighted her taste buds.

Missing her beloved cat, Lucky, Rachael wondered if her cousins had any pets. To her delight, she met Luigi, a small black and white dog who greeted her with friendliness. Playing fetch with Luigi brought her immense joy.

The day continued with a visit to an ice cream shop, where Rachael treated herself to creamy chocolate ice cream, savoring each delightful bite. Upon returning home, dinner featured delicious pizza, spaghetti and meatballs, and a plate of delectable cheese and bread.

As the evening unfolded, Rachael watched her relatives crochet, a skill she had learned from her mother. Eventually, exhaustion caught up with her, and she yawned, signaling that it was time for bed.

Rachael's time spent with her distant relatives created cherished memories that she would hold dear. When the time came to bid farewell and head back home, Rachael felt a mix of emotions.

While she was eager to reunite with Lucky, she couldn't help but wonder when her relatives would visit her and what exciting adventures awaited her in the future.

www.ingramcontent.com/pod-product-compliance
Lightning Source LLC
Chambersburg PA
CBHW042356070526
44585CB00028B/2955